# Welcome to Busy Book 2!

Find the items hidden in the book.

The Busy Book helps children develop in the following areas of learning…

 **Communication** — Learning to speak together in English.

 **Movement** — Being active and building confidence.

 **Finding out** — Learning about and exploring the world.

 **Critical thinking** — Solving problems and puzzles and learning thinking skills.

 **Creativity** — Expressing ideas through drawing and making.

 **We can do it!** — Celebrating learning and progress.

# 1 Let's explore together

Polar Polly

Jungle Joe

**Trace and circle**

Polar Polly has:

sneakers / glasses

Jungle Joe has a:

scarf / cap

Find. Check (✓) or put an X.

Polar Polly   Jungle Joe

 belt  ◯ ◯
 watch ◯ ◯
 scarf ◯ ◯
 sneakers ◯ ◯

# The Scarecrow

Look, the scarecrow has a cap.

Look, the scarecrow has a cap and a scarf.

Look, the scarecrow has a cap, a scarf, and a coat.

color me

Look, the scarecrow has a friend.

In the last picture, why is the scarecrow happy?

# Let's create

Make an explorer.

**Choose and draw:**

What's your explorer called?

_____

**Say with me!**

It's long, it's short, it's blond, it's dark. What is it?

_____

Tell a friend about your explorer.

## Explore with Basil

# Our world

Match the hero to the badge.

Who's your hero?

**Basil's Fun Facts**

**Ask your family**
Who's your hero?

This is a *firefighter*.

# Make and act

### Find what you need

**1** Think and plan your accessory.

**2** Draw and cut.

**3** Make your accessory.

What do I have in my backpack? Guess.

Do you have a watch?

Yes, I do.

# Let's be happy at home

2

How many things starting with "t" can you find?

**Choose who lives here**

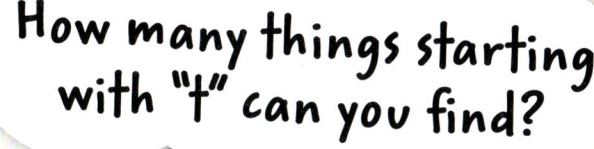

**Find and write.**

 It's in the  living room .

 It's in the _____.

 It's in the _____.

It's in the _____.

7

**Read with Clara** ▶ BB3

# Where's Kitty?

Where's Kitty?

She's in the yard, she's hot!

She's in the kitchen, she's sad! She's in the living room, she's cold!

color me

Do animals feel happy and sad? ✓ or ✗

Oh, she's in the bedroom, she's happy!

# Let's create

Imagine your perfect home.

Draw your perfect home.

**Say with me!**

There's a couch, a lamp, and a TV. Where am I?

_____

Tell a friend about your home.

# Make and play

**Find what you need**

**1** Think and plan your paper chain.

**2** Cut and write.

**3** Make your paper chain.

The lamp is next to the bed.

You're in the bedroom.

**What room am I in? Guess.**

# This is my farm

This is my farm, this is my farm,

come and look and see.

There isn't a cow,

There isn't an owl,

There isn't a goat or a sheep.

This is my farm, this is my farm,

come and look and see.

There is a donkey,

There is a turkey,

There is a mouse and a bee.

Color the animals that are at the farm.

**Explore with Basil**

# Our world

Match the pictures to the senses.

taste
◯
◯

see
◯
◯

hear
◯
◯

touch
◯
◯

What do you like to smell?

**Basil's Fun Facts**

Butterflies use their feet to taste.

**Ask your family**
What's your favorite smell?

15

# Make and play

### Find what you need

**1** Think about things you like to...

- see
- smell
- taste
- touch
- hear

**2** Find, cut, and draw.

**3** Make your sensory garden.

Draw and guess.

It's a cow!

# Let's try new activities

Spot the difference.

4

How many differences can you find?

6 7 8

## Match

fly · roller-skate · climb · ride · catch

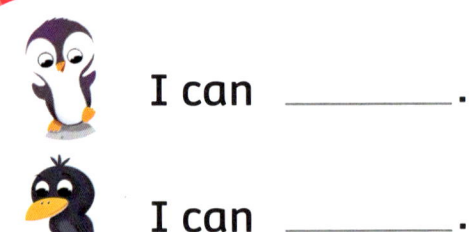

## Explore with Basil

# Our world

**Match the picture to the fact.**

keys

strings

holes

It has 4 strings.

It has 88 keys.

I can see 7 holes.

### Basil's Fun Facts

This is a harp.

**Listen to your favorite song. What instruments can you hear?**

**Ask your family** What instruments can you play?

# Make and play

### Find what you need

**1** Think and choose an instrument.

**2** Make your instrument.

**3** Play!

Would you like to play a board game?

What can you do with your friend? Choose and play.

# 5 Let's share our food

**Find**

- carrot
- cookie
- fish
- eggs
- juice
- cereal

How many things starting with "c" can you find?

22

**Read with Clara** ▶ BB6

# Busy in the kitchen

What are you doing in the kitchen?

I'm _____ the fruit.    I'm _____ eggs.    I _____ milkshakes.

Surprise! It's your birthday breakfast! Enjoy your special day, Mom.

What special day is it?
_____

**Explore with Basil**

# Our world

Match the food to where it's from.

Egg

Orange

Carrot

Carrot plant

Chicken

Orange tree

Check (✓) when you do each activity.

- Cooking food ◯
- Eating a snack ◯
- Washing your hands ◯
- Eating fruit ◯
- Growing a flower ◯
- Making a cake ◯

**Ask your family**
*What's your favorite juice?*

**Basil's Fun Facts**

Bananas grow on trees.

# Make and mime

**Find what you need**

1. Think and choose your food.

2. Make your snack.

3. Eat.

Ask an adult for help.

Mime and guess.

Are you eating a burger?

# I want to...

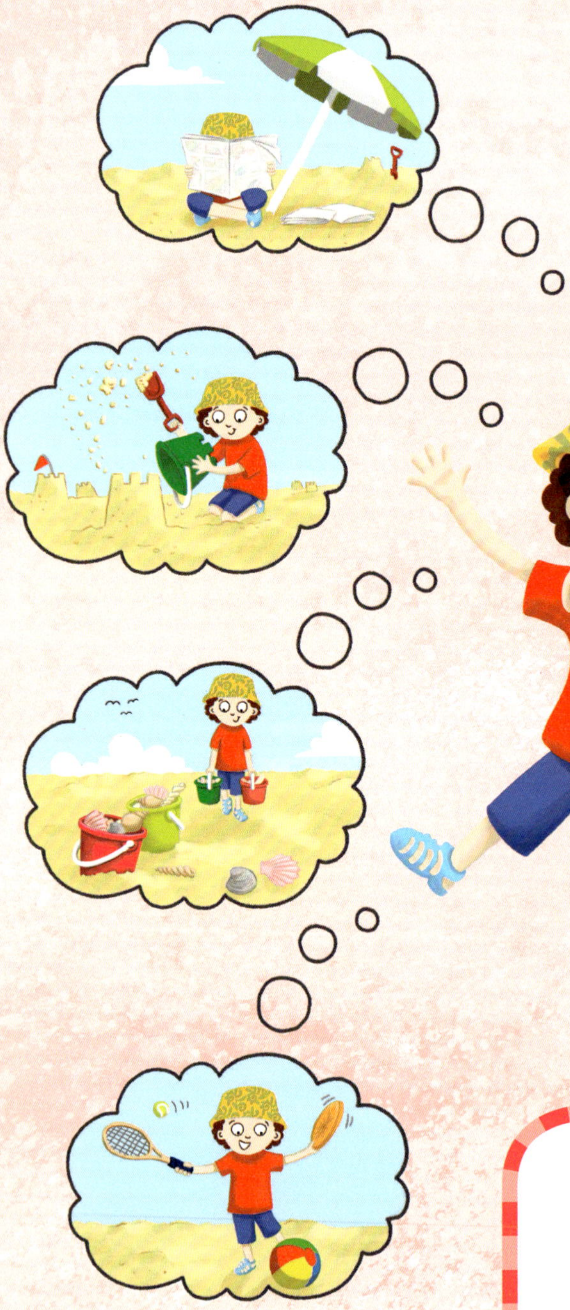

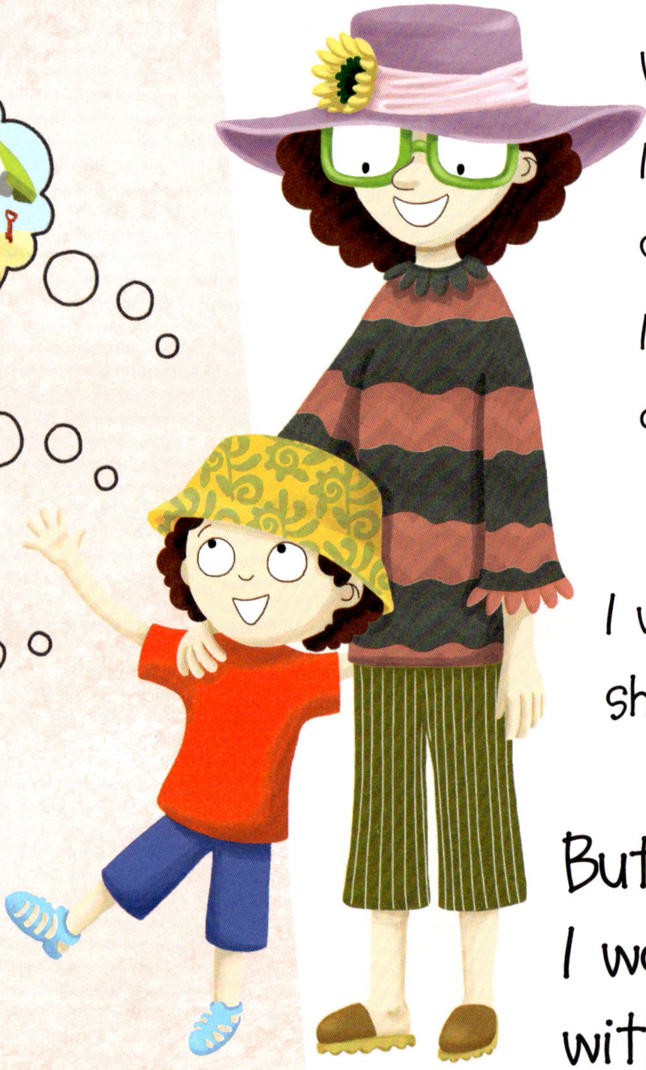

What do I want to do? I want to _____ comic books.

I want to _____ a sandcastle.

I want to _____ shells.

But most of all, I want to _____ with you.

The girl wants to _____.

And you?

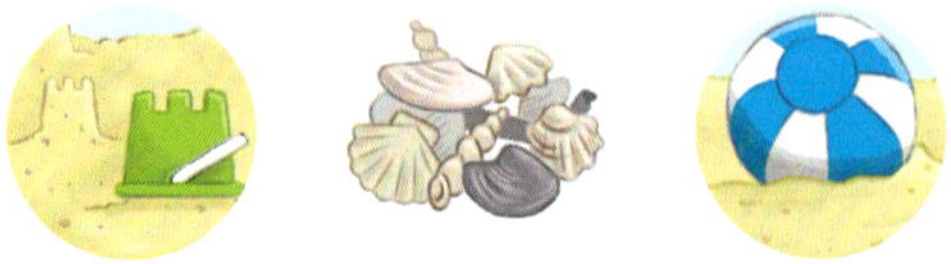

I want to _____.

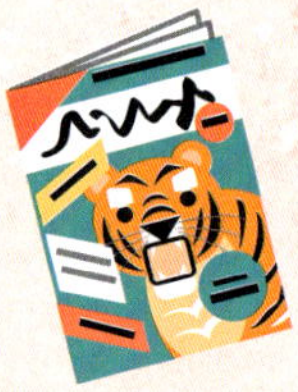

# Let's create

Play the game.

| Do you want to… | read comic books  | in the morning? |
| | build a sandcastle  | in the afternoon? |
| | collect shells  | in the evening? |
| | sleep  | at night? |

Purple, yellow.

Do you want to build a sandcastle in the morning?

Yes, I do.

**Say with me!**

She builds sacastndles

_____

Draw yourself doing the activity.

Write a sentence for your picture.

## Explore with Basil — Our world

Always ask an adult: "Is it safe to swim?"

What sign do you see every day?

Match the flags to the ocean.

I can see a red flag.
The ocean is _____.

I can see a green flag.
The ocean is _____.

**Ask your family**
Can you swim?

**Basil's Fun Facts**
A lifeguard can help you in the water.

# Make and say

**Find what you need**

1. Think and plan your Vacation fun poster.

2. Draw and cut.

3. Make your Vacation Fun poster.

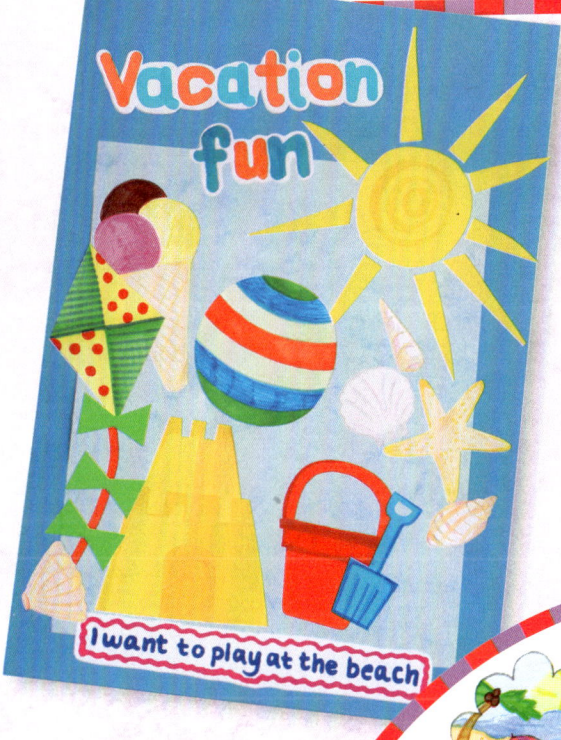

Imagine you're on vacation. Where do you want to go?

I want to go to the beach.

# Rise and Shine — Goodbye

## Rise and Shine Certificate

### You finished the book!
### Great work!

Awarded to: _____    Age: _____

| Oscar | Tess | Basil | Clara | Peanut |
|---|---|---|---|---|
| Oscar | Tess | Basil | Clara | 🐾 |